Bill Clinton:
Eyes on the Future

by

Leslie Kitchen

MARYLAND HISTORICAL PRESS
9205 Tuckerman Street
Lanham, MD   20706-2711

ISBN 0-917882-38-5 Hardcover
ISBN 0-917882-39-3 Paperback

Kitchen, Leslie, 1950-
    Bill Clinton : eyes on the future / by Leslie Kitchen.
        p.   cm.
    Includes bibliographical references and index.
    ISBN 0-917882-38-5 (Hardcover) : $17.50. -- ISBN 0-917882-39-3
(Pbk.) : $12.50
    1. Clinton, Bill, 1946-   . 2. Presidents--United States-
-Biography.   [1. Clinton, Bill, 1946-   . 2. Presidents.]
I. Title.
E886.K58   1994
973.929'092--dc20
    [B]   94-17298
                                                              CIP
                                                               AC

To the sweet memory of
my daughter Colette, and to
my daughter Michelle,
the inspirations for all that I am,
and all that I ever can be.

Photograph courtesy The White House.

William Jefferson "Bill" Clinton, president of the United States.

Table of Contents

Front cover photograph courtesy Jim Perry/*Hope Star*.
Back cover photograph courtesy The White House.

Type design by Linda Blachly.

Two-year-old Billy Blythe and his mother, Virginia, at
Christmas, 1948.

Chapter 1

First Steps

Billy Blythe, who later became President Bill Clinton, was born in Hope, Arkansas on August 19, 1946. No one guessed in that summer of 1946 that this newborn child would grow up to become the president of the United States. At that time, his prospects for the future seemed very limited, indeed. As it remains today, Arkansas, a land of enormous physical beauty, was one of the poorest states in all of the United States. In addition, Billy was born without a father to love him and provide for him. Three months before Billy's birth, his father, William Jefferson Blythe III, had been killed in an automobile accident. He had been thrown from his car and knocked unconscious. He drowned in a few inches of water in the middle of the night.

The fatherless child was to grow up to beat the odds. One very important reason for his future success was that he had the good fortune of being born to an unusually resourceful and determined woman.

Billy's mother, Virginia Blythe, knew that she and her son faced an uncertain future on her nurse's salary. She was determined to improve her situation. She felt that she needed to obtain a better job so she could provide for herself and her little boy. She had to do that without a husband to help her. She did not want her son to grow up and face hardship every day. That is why she decided to

G. Warren Sears, artist.

"I remember climbing the mountain of sawdust, how it smelled on those spring and summer nights — such a vivid memory."

increase her education by taking advanced nursing classes at a nursing school far away in New Orleans, Louisiana. She made that decision with her eyes on the future. She believed that education was the key to a better life for both herself and her son.

The decision to go away to nursing school was a difficult one because it meant leaving little Billy behind. Billy and his mother, however, were fortunate because she could leave him with her parents. Billy and his grandparents, Eldridge and Edith Cassidy, loved each other very much. He lived safely with them for the next four years. Virginia returned from New Orleans to see her young son as often as she could. Many tears were shed at the train station when they parted. President Clinton has said, "I remember my mother crying and actually falling down on her knees by the railbed . . . my grandmother was saying, 'She's doing this for you.'" [1]

Even though Billy missed his mother, life with his grandparents was often full of joy. His grandfather, a night watchman at an old sawmill, was one of Billy's favorite playmates. The long nights as a watchman were lonely for Eldridge Cassidy. That is why, after Billy became a little older, he was sometimes allowed to jump into the car with his granddad and off to the sawmill they would go. Billy would play late into the night at that sawmill. He would rush like an excited pup to the "sawdust mountain" where he would laugh and climb and play in the darkness until he was exhausted. In remembering those nights, Bill Clinton later said, "I remember climbing the mountain of sawdust, how it smelled on those spring and summer nights — such a vivid memory." [2]

3

Photograph courtesy the University of Arkansas, Elsaess Papers.

Just before Christmas, five-year-old Billy Blythe points to his stocking. Above his head are photographs showing his father, William Blythe, III, and his mother, Virginia Blythe.

4

In those important years before he started school, Billy's grandparents gave him special gifts. By the time he was three years old, his grandparents had taught him to count, to read little books, and even to read newspapers. They also encouraged Billy to read the Bible. Just as they had taught Billy's mother, they repeated to him again and again that learning was the key to getting ahead in life. They taught him to keep his eyes on the future. Billy was bright, energetic, and eager to please those who loved him. Right from the start, he seemed just as eager to learn as he was to climb that giant sawdust mountain!

Because of the love that surrounded him, Billy's childhood was a carefree existence that enabled him to grow up healthy and happy. Like many children who spend a lot of time with their grandparents, Billy became used to being the center of attention.

Billy racing down the sidewalk on his tricycle, decked out in cowboy boots and cowboy hat, was a familiar sight to those who lived nearby. Joe Purvis, who is now an attorney, went to kindergarten with Billy and lived only four blocks from Billy's home. He remembers evenings spent running shirtless and barefoot across the thick grass, chasing after Billy and the other kids or catching lightning bugs. [3]

During that time, Billy's grandfather managed to save enough money to start a small grocery store. The store was in the poorest part of town. Many times, customers did not have the money to pay. Billy's grandfather, however, allowed his customers to take what they needed if they would promise to pay him later. Billy saw his grandfather sell many items that way to both

Bill Clinton's boyhood homes in Hope, Arkansas.

black and white customers.

President Bill Clinton now says that he learned many lessons in that store. He learned that all people should be treated fairly. [4] He also learned how important it is for parents to be able to provide what their families need. By watching his grandparents and their customers, Billy learned about kindness and trust. He developed a deep belief that every person deserves a chance to be a success in life.

When Billy was four years old, his mother married again. Her new husband's name was Roger Clinton. Roger was now Billy's stepfather and Billy was glad to have a brand-new dad. Billy Blythe soon became known around town as Billy Clinton.

When Billy was seven years old, the Clinton family moved to a new life in a much larger town, Hot Springs, Arkansas. For a little boy from a small town, Hot Springs must have seemed very large and exciting. Every day in his new city must have been an adventure!

In the middle of the 1950s, television was coming into millions of American homes for the first time. Because of that, Americans were able to learn more about the world than ever before. When Billy was nine years old, the Clinton family bought its first television set. That television opened up the world to Billy. It helped him to learn new and interesting things. He was especially excited to watch the presidential election in 1956. Billy paid close attention both because the conventions were so exciting and dramatic and because he was always hungry to learn.

Photograph courtesy Hot Springs Chamber of Commerce.

Hot Springs, Arkansas, the small city in which Bill Clinton grew to manhood.

Photo courtesy David Leopoulos.

Billy Clinton and two of his childhood pals (about fifth grade). He was about 10 years old.

Billy's home at 213 Scully Street became a meeting place for him and his friends. Billy's mother was a great favorite among Billy's friends because she took them seriously. She often started debates among the children, daring them to think on their own. Recalling those years she has said, "I'd make cocoa, and we'd just sit around the dining room table and talk. Those 'kids' are now middle-aged, and I'll bet every one of them would say how wonderful it was to talk to a parent without a TV blaring in the background." [5]

David Leopoulos, one of his closest boyhood friends, loved spending time at Billy's house. When the two were not playing touch football in Billy's large backyard, they could usually be found inside playing Monopoly™, card games or listening to Elvis Presley records. Sometimes the boys hiked through the mountains near Hot Springs, exploring the rock quarries and enjoying the beautiful scenery. Mr. Leopoulos, who now works as a computer software salesman, recalls those times he spent with Billy as a "very Huckleberry Finnish kind of deal." [6]

In those years, Billy's family had many good times together. But the Clinton family had some bad times, too. Billy's family had a big problem because his stepfather was an alcoholic. When he drank too much, Roger Clinton would sometimes get loud and mean. Billy's mother often feared for herself and her son. Virginia and Roger Clinton split up several times because of the family's big problem. Once Billy even saw his drunken stepfather angrily fire a gun in their home. The bullet made an ugly hole in the wall that today President Clinton says he still has not forgotten. He would later recall: "I remember the police coming and taking him away. That was a pretty

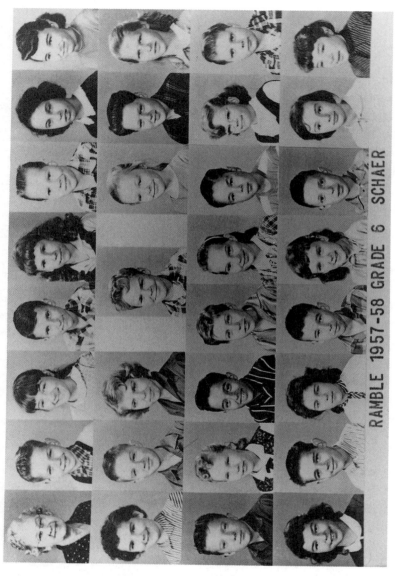

Photo courtesy David Leopoulos.

The sixth grade class at Ramble Elementary School in Hot Springs, Arkansas (1957-58). Billy Clinton, age 11, is second from the right, second row.

10

spooky deal." [7]

Billy tried to pay as little attention as possible to the problems at home. He certainly did not talk about them, even with his closest friends. David Leopoulos now says that he believes young Clinton could not talk about anything negative that was going on in his family. As a candidate for the presidency, Clinton told *Newsweek:* "I didn't know I was supposed to talk about it. I was raised . . . where you put on a happy face, and you didn't reveal your pain and agony." [8]

Billy handled the problem and avoided it as much as possible by spending a lot of time at church and at school, staying busy with as many activities as possible. Staying so busy enabled him to develop a great knack for meeting and speaking with both adults and other young people. Billy made friends wherever he went. Some youngsters thought everything came easy for Billy Clinton. He did not talk about his problems. He was successful and popular. He seemed perfect.

But no child can be perfect. For example, Billy developed a deep love for talking. That was a good thing, but Billy loved to talk even when he was supposed to be quiet. For example, one day while in grade school, he brought home a report card that was nearly all A's. The only bad mark was a D in conduct. Billy's mom went straight to the school to find out why her son had received such a poor grade. The teacher told her that Billy was very eager to do well and always knew the answers to her questions. The problem was that he would not give the other children a chance to answer. Billy would always shout out the answer, even when it was someone else's turn.

SYGMA photograph.

Two grade school photographs of Billy Clinton.

Billy's teacher knew that Billy was eager to please and that the D in conduct would make him want to improve. [9] Billy did improve, but he never lost his love for talking.

When Billy was old enough to go to high school, he continued to study hard to get high grades in every subject. Even though he spent a lot of time studying, he was always willing to make time to help his mother care for his little brother, Roger, Jr. Billy liked being a big brother. Also, just as he had been trained from the start, he continued to go to Sunday School every Sunday.

Somehow Billy also found time to play the saxophone in his high school band. He even played in his own musical group called "Three Blind Mice." Before too long, Billy became recognized as one of the finest high school saxophone players in all of Arkansas. He was also a member of several civic groups.

Billy Clinton had a very busy life. Only a very competitive person, one who yearned for recognition, would have kept such a busy schedule. Carolyn Staley, one of Bill Clinton's closest friends, has summed up those years of his life by saying, "He had to be the class leader. He had to be the best in the band. He had to be the best in the class, in grades. And he wanted to be in the top of anything that put him in the forefront of any course." [10] Edith Irons, the guidance counselor at Billy's Hot Springs High School, has said: "I don't know how he could be on the band field at six a.m. and be back at school and go, go, go all day." [11] Even President Clinton today has said that when he was young he thought he was busier than anyone he knew.

13

Keeping so busy helped Billy forget about his family's big problem. But avoiding the big problem did not make it go away. Once, when he was fourteen years old, he heard his stepfather yelling at his mother in their bedroom. Bill was now nearly a full-grown man and felt that he could not allow this any longer. He charged into the room to defend his mother. Angrily, he told his stepfather that he was never to harm anyone in the family again. Bill Clinton took a big step that day. He was growing up in a hurry.

SYGMA photograph/Mike Stewart.

Bill Clinton, his mother Virginia and his younger brother, Roger Clinton, Jr.

Photograph courtesy Hot Springs, Arkansas Chamber of Commerce.

The Hot Springs High School where Bill Clinton learned many early lessons in leadership.

Photograph courtesy David Leopoulos.

Bill Clinton with David Leopoulos, clowning around at a high school variety show.

16

Chapter 2

Climbing

Life was a lot easier for Bill at school than at home. Early in life, he developed a talent for leadership. Nearly all who met young Bill Clinton were impressed with his energy, his confidence and his friendly ways. His high school teachers and classmates came to admire him very much. Carolyn Staley, Bill's next-door neighbor and classmate, remembers him as poised and seeming much older and more serious than his classmates. The teachers at Hot Springs High School encouraged the students to develop their leadership abilities and to serve their country. Bill listened and decided that public service was a good and honorable activity. [1]

Bill's reputation as a young leader grew quickly. He was a member of Demolay, president of his Kiwanis Key Club and president of the Beta Club, a scholastic honor society. He was recognized for his abilities by being selected to attend a make-believe government called Boy's State. Carolyn Staley was selected to attend Girl's State. From there, he and Carolyn were selected to represent Arkansas at Boy's Nation and Girl's Nation.

Bill and Carolyn were rewarded with trips to Washington, D.C. They even had the opportunity to shake hands with President John F. Kennedy! Carolyn Staley

17

Photograph courtesy The White House.

Shaking hands with President Kennedy was the high point of Bill Clinton's trip to Washington, D.C.

18

remembers all that as a deeply satisfying and happy time. She says that she and Bill were very proud of each other in a quiet way and that "there was a lot of smiling and basking in the afterglow." [2]

Shaking hands with President Kennedy was the most exciting thing that had ever happened to Bill! After that, Bill began to dream of a political career. He dreamed of working in politics with people from many different countries. Bill wanted to make the world a better place to live for everyone.

Recalling his decision to become a politician, Bill Clinton would later say: " When I was 16, I decided if I had a chance I would go into politics. I had been interested in being a musician, a physician or a politician. While I was very good at music, I would never be great. In politics, I thought I had unique abilities — I was genuinely interested in people and in solving problems. It was something I could be good at, something I could love." [3] All of that would require sacrifice. It would mean long hours of work while others were taking it easy.

Bill started making his dreams come true just after it was suggested to him that he attend college at Georgetown University in Washington, D.C. He had fallen in love with the nation's capital the year before when he had met President Kennedy. Georgetown University became the only place he wanted to go to college. It even became hard to fall asleep at night. Perhaps the excitement and happiness that he felt made him remember a joyous little boy who laughed in the Arkansas moonlight as he charged for the top of a sawdust mountain.

Georgetown University accepted Bill and gave him a scholarship. When he arrived at Georgetown, he continued to work hard. He continued to show the tremendous leadership ability his teachers had nurtured in him at Hot Springs High School. In fact, he ran for president of his class during both his first and second years in college and was elected both times.

Just before his sophomore year, Bill found himself running low on cash. Attending Georgetown University was expensive and Bill did not come from a wealthy family. He was afraid that he might not be able to continue his education at the school he had come to love.

Bill knew he could solve most of his money problems if he could manage to land a job working in the nation's capital as an assistant for Senator J. William Fulbright. Bill was told that there was one full-time job available at $5,000 per year. He was also told that there were two part-time jobs available that paid $3,000 per year. Bill, thinking quickly, shot back that he would take the two part-time jobs. Senator Fulbright's office hired Bill, enabling him to remain in school. This work also provided the eager youngster with his first close-up look at how government operates on a daily basis.

In spite of working many hours each week, Bill continued to excel in his classes. Tom Campbell, Bill's roommate for four years at Georgetown, recalls that one of Bill's secrets of success was that he was able to work both steadily and in great bursts. According to Campbell, Bill would often work late into the night and would have time only for two or three hours of sleep. He would make up for his lack of sleep the next day by catching several

Photograph courtesy Tom Campbell.

Some friends with Bill Clinton at a party at Georgetown
University, 1968. Bill graduated three months later.

21

twenty-minute naps. After each nap, he would get up refreshed and ready to go. Campbell remembers Bill as a young man who was able to organize his time very well and always planned to do the most important things first. According to Campbell, Bill had a deep belief that education was the road to worldly success, that Bill believed very much ". . . that education could get you from where you are to where you want to be." [4]

Bill also worked tirelessly to meet and talk at length with anyone who could broaden his view of life, especially anyone who could teach him how our giant government in Washington works. Carolyn Staley claims that even before Bill went off to college, he always showed an intense interest in meeting people. She says that whenever her family would have guests from out of town, as when her aunt and uncle visited from Pennsylvania, Bill would pop over, showing no shyness whatever, and would engage them in friendly conversation. [5]

Bill continued those friendly, easygoing ways throughout his years at Georgetown. He still had tremendous ability and enthusiasm for meeting people. In that way, Bill had not changed since grade school. Tom Campbell maintains that Bill Clinton was never the small-town boy lost in the big city. "He would talk to anybody . . . People were his coin," Campbell recalls. [6]

In 1967 Bill was faced with a hard decision. His stepfather, Roger Clinton, Sr., was dying from cancer at Duke University Hospital in Durham, North Carolina. Even though there had been bitterness and tension between Bill and his stepfather, he was the only father Bill had ever known. Bill still loved and respected him. That is why each week for six weeks, Bill made the 550-mile round trip between Washington, D.C. and Durham, North Carolina to see his dying stepfather.

Bill's visits eased his stepfather's loneliness. They talked about old times, played card games, and Bill helped Roger, Sr. get around his hospital room. The visits in those last weeks before his stepfather's death gave them the chance to grow closer and to express the love and tenderness they felt for each other. Roger Clinton, Sr. died knowing that his stepson had grown into a fine young man.

Back at Georgetown University, Bill continued to excel in his classes. His years of hard work paid off when he received a special award. It was a Rhodes Scholarship to study at Oxford University in England, one of the most important universities in the world. The eager and bookish little boy from the small town of Hope, Arkansas had come a long way. Abraham Lincoln's law partner once said of our sixteenth president that his desire to get ahead in life was a "little engine" that knew no rest. Bill Clinton was an extremely ambitious young man with an "engine" much like Abraham Lincoln's.

Bill appreciated the wonderful education offered by Oxford University. Since all of his expenses were paid by his scholarship, he did not have to work to support himself as he had done at Georgetown. Bill had become used to organizing his time tightly. The slower pace of Oxford University offered the energetic young man the opportunity to read widely, to travel and to meet with other brilliant students from all over the world.

After two years at Oxford, Bill returned to the

23

United States to attend law school at Yale University. He knew that going to law school was an important step that would help him reach his dream of a career in public service. Once again, this meant long hours of study while working at two and sometimes three part-time jobs. While at Yale, Bill taught at a small community college. He also worked for a Hartford city councilman and for an attorney.

Even though Bill was still very young, he had already learned in his life that good things cannot be obtained without effort. He had learned that from his mother. He had learned it from his grandparents. He had learned it from the teachers he had looked up to during his years in school. They had taught him to sacrifice today so that tomorrow would bring better things. They had taught him to keep his eyes on the future.

But all was not to be study and work for Bill Clinton. One night in the library at Yale, he noticed a lovely girl across the room. She looked serious and was busy with her work. Bill pretended to study, but he kept glancing at her. The usually talkative, and not shy, Bill Clinton found himself simply staring at the pretty young woman. Finally, she walked right over to him and introduced herself! Her name, she told him, was Hillary Rodham. This surprised Bill so much that he couldn't answer. He couldn't even remember his own name! These two went on to become good friends and, before long, Bill Clinton and Hillary Rodham fell in love.

With the help of late-night study sessions, often with Hillary at his side, Bill went on to receive his law degree at Yale in 1973. Now was the time for a big decision. He could stay in the northeast and earn a lot of money, but Bill

Bill Clinton, age 26, and others welcomed U.S. Senator Barry Goldwater when the former presidential candidate (1964) visited Arkansas in 1972.

missed his home state. It had been many years since he had lived in Arkansas, a land of great natural beauty. That was where he had grown up. That was where his family lived. That was where his oldest and dearest friends lived. He even missed the fried pies and gigantic watermelons that seemed to be available only in his home state.

Also, Bill knew that although Arkansas was a land of great natural resources, it remained a very poor state. He wanted to use all the things he had learned to help build a better future for Arkansas. That is why Bill decided to go back home. He loaded up his car and went back to the places and people he loved.

Chapter 3

Charging for the Top

After Bill returned home from Yale, he taught at the University of Arkansas in Fayetteville. Before long, in 1974, he decided to run for a seat in the U.S. Congress as the Democratic candidate. Young Clinton ran in opposition to the war in Vietnam. He also criticized the administration of President Richard M. Nixon for its involvement in the Watergate burglary coverup.

Bill lost a close election to the very popular John Paul Hammerschmidt. Even though he lost the election, Bill gained a lot of attention. Many voters took notice of his youthful energy and his obvious leadership abilities. That election marked Bill Clinton as a young man who was a rising political star.

Losing was a disappointment to Bill, but it did not slow his life down one bit! He went on with his life. He had already persuaded Hillary Rodham to come to Arkansas. One day Bill took Hillary for a ride in his car and stopped in front of a small glazed-brick house at 930 California Blvd. in Fayetteville. Bill told Hillary that he had just finished buying the house because she had once told him that she liked it. Feeling a little braver than he had that first night he had met her at Yale, Bill said, "So I guess we'll have to get married now." [1] Some of Hillary's

27

Photograph courtesy Fayetteville, Arkansas, Chamber of Commerce.

It was here that Bill Clinton proposed marriage to Hillary Rodham. This house became their first home.

friends had thought that she had made a big mistake in following Bill to Arkansas. Yet, when she remembers it now, Hillary says, "Following your heart is never wrong."[2]

They were married on October 11, 1975. Bill now had a partner in his life. He and Hillary were both young and both of them had the energy to do important and exciting things. They were keenly intelligent and willing to work very hard for what they thought was right. They made a terrific team.

The next time Bill ran for office, he won. He ran for attorney general of the state of Arkansas in 1976 and served a successful two-year term in that office. After this, Bill Clinton had to decide what the next big step would be. More than anything else in the world at that time, Bill wanted to be governor of Arkansas, but he was still a very young man. He knew that many people would believe that he was too young for the job. He decided not to worry about that and to just do it, for he knew he had spent his whole life working hard to prepare himself for such an important job.

Young Bill Clinton ran for governor of the state of Arkansas in 1978 and won. He was only 32 years old. That made him the youngest governor in any of the fifty states.

But no one wins at everything he tries. Life is sometimes hard. For example, in 1980, when Bill ran for his second term as governor, he lost. Many people believed Bill had made some serious mistakes and they voted against him. They were angry because Bill had raised the prices on license plates for their cars and trucks.

Arkansas Democrat-Gazette photograph.

Hillary Clinton looked on as Bill Clinton took the oath of office for his first term (1978) as governor of Arkansas.

Arkansas Democrat-Gazette photograph.

A children's orchestra provided entertainment during the celebration of Governor Clinton's first inauguration (1978).

Many thought it seemed that Bill didn't even act like he was from Arkansas anymore. They even resented the fact that Hillary, contrary to tradition, had not taken her husband's last name and was called Hillary Rodham. Most of all, however, it seemed to many Arkansas voters that Bill was not a good listener.

Losing that election was a bitter disappointment for Bill. He let it drag him down for a while, but he did not stay down. The things that people were saying could not hold him back from trying again. Bill decided to show that he could be a good listener and that he could learn from his mistakes. He even had the courage to apologize to the people of Arkansas. He told the voters: "I made a young man's mistake. . . ." Later, he added: "I was so busy doing what I wanted to do that I didn't leave enough time to correct mistakes." [3] Many people respected that, even some of those who had voted against him. Bill showed that he could still grow.

Bill went on to be elected governor of Arkansas for two-year terms in 1982 and 1984, and for four-year terms in 1986 and 1990. Bill Clinton was able to win those elections because, many say, he became one of the best governors Arkansas ever had. Between 1978 and 1990, Bill was elected to serve as governor five times. No one has ever been elected governor of Arkansas more times than that.

It was in 1980, at the end of Bill's first term as governor, that a brand-new Clinton came along. A hospital worker at that time told a newspaper reporter that Bill was very excited on the night of his daughter's birth and that Bill " . . . walked all over the area last night holding the

31

Photograph courtesy Steve Smith.

Clinton was one of the youngest governors in any of the fifty states. Shown here in March 1979 with young Caleb Smith, son of Steve Smith, who was an aide to Clinton during his first term as governor of Arkansas.

Arkansas Democrat-Gazette photograph.

Governor Clinton and several Arkansas schoolchildren took this opportunity to keep their state clean.

Photograph courtesy *Northwest Arkansas Times.*

Governor Clinton on a tour of Leverett Elementary School, Fayetteville, Arkansas (1989).

baby in his arms." [4]   As he held his little girl, Bill was deeply moved, because he knew that he had never been held by his own father. [5]   A family friend says he remembers Bill walking around the hospital room holding his newborn daughter and acting as though he had just invented fatherhood. Hillary and Bill recalled a song they loved called "Chelsea Morning." Chelsea was the name they chose for their daughter.

Little Chelsea filled her parents' home with love and changed their lives forever. Their new baby was a great responsibility. Bill was already busy with his duties as governor. Hillary, too, worked outside their home. She was a very successful attorney and had her own burning ambitions. She worked long hours at her job. In addition, she was also busy helping Bill improve the state of Arkansas.

Yet, though they were often tired out at the end of a long day's work, Bill and Hillary still made time to play with Chelsea every day and to take good care of her. The young couple found themselves working harder than they had ever worked before. They did all of these things because they wanted only the best from life for both themselves and the little girl they loved so much.

While Bill was governor of Arkansas, the Clinton family lived in the Governor's Mansion in Little Rock, the state capital. Although the red-brick colonial-style house is very large, the upstairs family living quarters are rather small. Luckily, Bill had a small family. Bill would say with a big grin that his was a small family, but a powerful one. The Clintons thought their cozy home was just fine.

Arkansas Democrat-Gazette photograph.

Hillary, Bill and Chelsea Clinton are shown here with Donald Duck, enjoying a Florida vacation at Disney World.

Photographs courtesy *Northwest Arkansas Times*.

In 1989, Governor Clinton joined with students to help them celebrate the 100th anniversary of Leverett Elementary School.

Photograph courtesy the Arkansas Democratic Party.

From the beginning, Bill and Hillary Clinton have made a very effective political team.

The Clinton family had unusually busy lives and the years passed quickly by. Before long Chelsea was off to public school. In the evenings after school, Hillary and Chelsea would rush out for some quick grocery shopping. When they returned home, Governor Bill would whip up supper. He was very proud of his specialty — omelettes for everybody! After supper, the little family would gather around a table for a game of Hearts or Gin Rummy in the combined living room and dining room. Each one played to win, especially Chelsea, who loved to beat her parents. Later, after Chelsea was in bed, the governor would often work at his desk late into the night. Sometimes, exhausted from the day's work, he would relax by reading a mystery novel or by solving a crossword puzzle.

Friends usually came over on weekends to visit the governor and his family. Everyone would talk, relax and have a good time. They knew that wherever Bill Clinton was there was always a lot of talk. Chelsea would sometimes join in and tell everyone about her schoolwork, her ballet lessons and her softball and volleyball teams. In a teasing way, Chelsea would frequently complain about her father's behavior at her softball games. It seems that Bill would get excited and would jump up and down on the bleachers, wave his arms and yell so much that everyone stared at him. Chelsea knew her father did these things out of love and pride but she was shy and easily embarrassed.

After Hillary and Chelsea were in bed the talk would often go on late into the night. Bill and his friends would stop only to raid the refrigerator around midnight. Then they would gather around the snack bar to continue their lively discussions of sports, politics, traveling, books, movies and many other things. Governor Bill Clinton and his family worked hard but they played hard, too!

During those years of hard work and good times, Governor Clinton helped realize many advances for Arkansas, the state he loved so much. He had once told Hillary, "I promised myself a long time ago, if the people of Arkansas will let me, I'll break my back to help my state. . . . That's my life. And that's the way it has to be for me." [6]

For example, Bill convinced many business leaders from other states to move their businesses to Arkansas. Many people in Arkansas were able to get jobs because of that. Those jobs helped many families have the things they needed. Bill had learned how important that was in those early years in his grandfather's store. Also, the young governor created government programs that helped small-farm owners. This in turn helped small businesses to survive and grow.

Governor Clinton also wanted very much for every child to be able to go to a good school. He knew how important education had been in his own success. He also knew that a large investment in the entire school system was needed so that Arkansas could one day grow out of its poverty. When he first became governor, he found the schools in Arkansas suffering from years of neglect. Arkansas was spending less on the education of each student than any other state. Teachers were very poorly paid. The governor believed that not nearly enough students were going on to college.

Governor Clinton attacked these problems head on. He set up a committee to find better ways of running the

Photograph courtesy Tom Campbell.

On the lawn of the Governor's Mansion in Little Rock, Arkansas, left-hander Bill Clinton delivers the pitch as Ciara Campbell prepares to give it a good whack.

41

Arkansas Democrat-Gazette photograph.

From the very start of his time as governor of Arkansas, Bill Clinton showed a strong interest in the problems of children.

Photograph courtesy *Northwest Arkansas Times.*

Governor Clinton on a visit to the Arkansas and Missouri Railroad during the 1990 campaign for governor.

Arkansas Democrat-Gazette photograph.

As governor, Bill Clinton worked hard to see that each Arkansas child received a good education.

schools in the state. He appointed his wife Hillary to lead the committee. Hillary and the other committee members traveled all through the state, to all of its seventy-five counties, talking to teachers and parents. The information they gathered helped create new ideas for education in Arkansas. Governor Clinton increased spending on education by 40 percent. He raised the pay of teachers. Governor Clinton summed up the new ideas when he reminded the voters that the kids of Arkansas deserved a "blue-ribbon" education. Everyone in the state was encouraged to wear a blue ribbon in support of the governor's changes.

Governor Clinton also used his power to improve the lives of black people in Arkansas. His religious upbringing had taught him to believe that all persons are equal in God's sight. During his terms of office, Governor Bill Clinton acted on those beliefs and appointed more black people to jobs in the state government than had all the previous Arkansas governors combined. He also supported a state civil rights bill that was an attempt to guarantee blacks and other minorities an equal chance to find jobs. The bill was defeated by the legislature, however, and did not become law.

Not everyone, of course, thought Bill Clinton had done a great job. He had many political enemies. Some pointed out that while he was in office the state's natural environment, especially the beautiful waterways, had become fouled by pollution. It was also said that Governor Clinton paid for his reforms with increased sales taxes that took money out of the pockets of many who were already very poor.

Arkansas Democrat-Gazette photograph.

Bill Clinton addressed an eager crowd just after filing his name with the state of Arkansas as candidate for his fifth term as governor.

Yet, it can fairly be said that Governor Clinton and his ideas helped make Arkansas a better place to live. By creating jobs, and by improving education and race relations, the Clinton administration was successful. Because of that, Bill's reputation grew. In 1988, at a meeting of the National Governor's Association, Governor Rudy Perpich of Minnesota presented Bill with a plaque honoring him for his leadership. Presenting the award, Governor Perpich called Bill the best governor in the United States. Many observers even spoke of the young Arkansas governor as a potential candidate for the presidency of the United States.

Photograph courtesy Jim Perry/*Hope Star*.

Bill Clinton in Hope, Arkansas, during the 1992 campaign for the presidency.

Chapter 4

Reaching the Peak

In 1991, Governor Bill Clinton had a difficult decision to make. He had a chance to run for the presidency of the United States in 1992. On the one hand, he knew he might never have another chance to seek the nation's highest office. On the other hand, he knew that the presidency would be the biggest and hardest job any man could have. Also, the campaign would take him away from his family for long periods of time.

In making his decision, Bill thought about all the years he had spent studying in school. He also thought about all the years he had served as governor of Arkansas. It seemed to him that he had spent his entire life preparing himself for such a moment, and he believed that he was ready.

First, Bill talked about the decision with Hillary and eleven-year-old Chelsea. Bill warned Chelsea that running for the presidency would not be easy, that people would say many nasty things about him. Chelsea, a little tougher than her father expected, piped back: "Dad they always say terrible things about you. You ought to go to my school. You can't imagine the things they say. You just got to blow it off and go on." [1]

Bill and Hillary Clinton worked together on the campaign trail.

Bill took his daughter's advice. On October 3, 1991, on the steps of the Old State House in Little Rock, Arkansas, he announced to the American people that he was a candidate for the presidency of the United States. He said, "We must provide the answers . . . the solutions. Make no mistake — this election is about change: change in our party, change in our national leadership, and change in our country. That is our challenge in 1992." Later in that same speech he said, "Together I believe we can provide leadership that will restore the American Dream — that will fight for the forgotten middle class — that will provide more opportunity, demand more responsibility, and create a greater sense of community for this great country." [2]

The campaign was off to a good start. Despite Bill's strongest efforts, however, things did not always go smoothly. During the New Hampshire primary campaign, rumors flew that he had in the past been unfaithful to his wife. He was also accused of having demonstrated in the 1970s against American involvement in the war in Vietnam. In addition, some old records seemed to indicate that when he was a student at Oxford, Bill had taken steps to avoid being drafted into the United States Army. Later on in the campaign, it even came out that when he was a student at Oxford, he had once smoked marijuana.

Bill fought back with great political skill. He agreed that he had been against the war in Vietnam. He denied, however, that he had ever made any underhanded or illegal moves to avoid military service. Bill defended himself most dramatically when he and Hillary appeared together on national television. The two of them insisted that they had a strong marriage and that they loved and respected each other. Later in the campaign, Bill said that he had

51

Arkansas Democrat-Gazette photograph.

The 1992 Democratic party running mates, Governor Bill Clinton of Arkansas and U.S. Senator Al Gore of Tennessee.

Arkansas Democrat-Gazette photograph.

Many people believed that attractive and able Hillary Rodham Clinton was a very valuable asset to Bill Clinton during the 1992 presidential campaign.

once smoked marijuana. He claimed that doing so was a youthful mistake and that it had never become a habit or a personal problem.

As the 1992 primary campaigns wore on, Bill Clinton of Arkansas began to emerge as the likely Democratic Party candidate for the presidency. On Super Tuesday, March 10, 1992, Clinton became the clear front-runner with victories in Florida, Louisiana, Mississippi, Oklahoma, Tennessee and Texas. This was followed by smashing successes in the Michigan and Illinois primaries that very nearly sewed up the nomination of the Democratic Party.

So, in the summer of 1992, Bill was chosen at the Democratic Convention to be his party's candidate in the presidential election. Bill selected Senator Albert Gore, Jr. of Tennessee to be his running mate as the Democratic candidate for the vice-presidency. In his speech accepting his party's nomination, Bill said, "Opportunity. Responsibility. Community. When we pull together America will pull ahead." [3]

After the convention, Bill had to run against President George Bush, the Republican candidate, and H. Ross Perot, a very wealthy businessman. After a while, nearly everyone could see that it came to a choice between Bill and President Bush.

President Bush, however, was not going to give up easily. He genuinely believed he was the better man for the job and said that American voters ought to re-elect him because of that. He reminded everyone that he has been president for four years. He said that although Americans

Photograph courtesy The White House.

Hillary Rodham Clinton.

were living in rough times, better days were ahead, and that Americans should be patient and give him four more years to solve the nation's problems. He also claimed that Bill Clinton had big ideas and big programs that would cost too much and that they would result in higher taxes.

Bill Clinton disagreed with President Bush that the voters should decide who was the better man. Bill wanted the voters to decide who had better ideas for America. Bill was full of ideas from his years at school. He had worked hard to get a first-rate education. He was at home with ideas and was able to think on his feet. He was also experienced from his long years of service as governor of Arkansas. He believed that if government were intelligently run by people of good will, it could be a force for good in the lives of all people.

That is why Bill tried to avoid spending too much time and effort arguing about who was the better man. He wanted to talk about his plans for America's future. He talked about those plans all over America. Bill Clinton had always loved to talk. He talked until his voice gave out. When his voice gave out, he tried to keep on talking. Bill's "little engine," just like Abraham Lincoln's, would not stop. He traveled across the entire nation, promising that he knew how to use the government to make everyone's life better.

Candidate Clinton ran on his record of success as governor of Arkansas. He maintained that he could create more jobs than President Bush could. Bill said that if Americans were going to be able to compete with people in other nations, America's children would have to have much better schools and that American workers needed better training. He promised to ease the tax burden of most

President-elect Clinton on election night, November 3, 1992. Al Gore, vice president-elect, and his wife are shown at left.

Americans and said he would require the wealthy to pay more. He also said that Americans, especially poor people, needed to be able to pay for the doctors and medicine necessary for healthy and productive lives.

After a while, it seemed that President Bush did not know how to fight back against all of Bill's ideas. On November 3, 1992, the American people chose Bill Clinton to be president of the United States. Americans decided to give the earnest, bright, and talkative candidate from Arkansas a chance to lead the nation. In his victory statement that night, Bill told Americans: "I accept tonight the responsibility that you have given me to be the leader of this, the greatest country in human history. I accept it with a full heart and a joyous spirit." [4]

Bill's dream had finally come true. His family and his friends had for many years believed that someday he could possibly become president of the United States. Bill had not let them down. He now had the biggest and hardest job in America. There were now opportunities to help build a better life for all Americans and to make the world a better and safer place to live. All of the years of hard work as a student and as a public servant had paid off one more time.

On January 20, 1993, Bill Clinton became the forty-second president of the United States. In his speech that day, President Clinton said that Americans must create a springtime in America. In that springtime, he said, we would be able to use bold new ideas to create a better America — an America that would have more liberty and justice for all. The president said that Americans could have those wonderful things if they learned to provide for

58

Photograph courtesy The White House.

Inauguration Day, January 20, 1993.

Clinton takes the Oath of Office, January 20, 1993, as
Hillary and Chelsea look on.

Photograph courtesy The White House.

President and First Lady Clinton enjoy dancing at an Inaugural Ball, January 20, 1993.

This young citizen made his feelings about Bill Clinton very clear.

their nation the way a family provides for its children.

That speech marked an inspiring beginning to a new chapter in American history. After that, Bill, Hillary, and Chelsea (and Socks, the family cat) moved into the White House in Washington D.C.

Right away, President Bill Clinton started doing what he loved to do the most. He began working hard so that his dreams for America's future would come true.

Photograph courtesy The White House.

Socks, Chelsea's cat, moved to Washington, D.C., too.

Sources

Interviews:
Carolyn Staley interview with the author, April 26, 1993.

David Leopoulos interview with the author, April 25, 1993.

Tom Campbell interview with the author, April 23, 1993.

Books:
Allen, Charles F., and Jonathan Portis, *The Comeback Kid: The Life and Career of Bill Clinton,* Birch Lane Press, 1992.

Dumas, Ernest, ed., *The Clintons of Arkansas: An Introduction by Those Who Know Them Best,* The University of Arkansas Press, Fayetteville, Arkansas, 1993.

Lerin, Robert E., *Bill Clinton: The Inside Story,* S.P.I. Books, New York, New York, 1992.

Moore, Jim and Rick Ihde, *Clinton: Young Man In a Hurry,* The Summit Group, Fort Worth Texas, 1992.

Osborne, David, *Laboratories of Democracy,* Harvard Business School Press, Cambridge, Massachusetts, 1988.

Articles:
Applebome, Peter, "Bill Clinton's Uncertain Journey," *New York Times Magazine,* March 8, 1992.

Ayres, Jr., B. Drummond, "Despite Improvements, the Schools in Arkansas are Still Among the Worst," *New York Times,* April 1, 1992.

Atler, Jonathan and Eleanor Clift, "You Don't Reveal Your Pain" (interview with Bill Clinton), *Newsweek,* March 30, 1992.

Baer, Donald, "Man-Child in Politics Land," *U.S. News & World Report,* October 14, 1991.

Baer, Donald, and Stephen V. Roberts, "The Making of Bill Clinton," *U.S. News & World Report,* March 30, 1992.

Baer, Donald, Matthew Cooper, and David R. Gergen, "Bill Clinton's Hidden Life," *U.S. News & World Report,* July 20, 1992.

Blumenthal, Sidney, "The Pol: Bill Clinton in Illinois," *The New Republic,* April 6, 1992.

Brinkley, Joel, "Clinton Remakes Home State in Own Image," *New York Times,* March 31, 1992.

Brooke, Jill, and Barbara Graustark, "At Home with Hillary Clinton," *Metropolitan Home,* November 1992.

Cooper, Matthew, "Clintons, Pea-Rows, and Piggly Wigglies," *U.S. News & World Report,* July 6, 1992.

Gerth, Jeff, "Policies Under Clinton are a Boon to Industry," *New York Times,* April 2, 1992.

Gleick, Elizabeth, "Hail to the Mom" (interview with Virginia Kelley, Bill Clinton's mother), *People,* November 16, 1992.

Holmes, Stephen A., "Race Relations in Arkansas Reflect Gains for Clinton, but Raise Questions," *New York Times,* April 3, 1992.

Jones, Landon Y., "Road Warriors," *People Weekly,* July 20, 1992.

Painton, Priscilla, "Clinton's Spiritual Journey," *Time,* April 5, 1993.

Payne, Lauren, "Inside the Governors' Mansions," *Ladies Home Journal,* July 1990.

Reed, Julia, "Clinton on the Brink," *Vogue,* June 1992.

Schneider, Karen S., and Garry Clifford, "Running Mate," *People Weekly,* February 17, 1992.

Schneider, Keith, "Clinton Relies on Voluntary Guidelines to Protect Environment in Arkansas," *New York Times,* April 4, 1992.

Stanley, Alexandra, "Most Likely to Succeed," *New York Times Magazine,* November 22, 1992.

Steele, Scott, "A Man of Hope," *Maclean's,* November 16, 1992.

Wills, Garry, "Beginning of the Road," *Time,* July 20, 1992.

Notes for Chapter 1

1. Quoted in *U.S. News and World Report,* October 14, 1991, page 40.

2. Quoted in *Time,* July 20, 1992, page 55.

3. See ed. Richard Dumas, *The Clintons of Arkansas: An Introduction by Those Who Know Them Best,* The University of Arkansas Press, Fayetteville, Arkansas, 1993, page 31.

4. "My commitment to civil rights was basically inbred through my grandparents, who ran a grocery store in a predominantly black neighborhood." Quoted in *U.S. News and World Report,* July 20, 1992, page 30.

5. From interview of Virginia Kelley by William Childress, *Ladies Home Journal,* February 1993.

6. From David Leopoulos interview with the author, April 25, 1993.

7. Quoted in *Time,* June 8, 1992, page 62.

8. Quoted in *Newsweek,* March 30, 1992, page 37.

9. See Charles F. Allen, *Bill Clinton: The Comeback Kid,* Birch Lane Press, New York, 1992, page 6.

10. Quoted in Allen, page 10.

11. Quoted in Jim Moore, *Clinton: Young Man in a Hurry,* The Summit Group, Fort Worth, Texas, page 24.

Notes for Chapter 2

1. From Carolyn Staley interview with the author, April 26, 1993.

2. From Carolyn Staley interview with the author, April 26, 1993.

3. Quoted in *U.S. News and World Report,* July 20, 1992.

4. From Tom Campbell interview with the author, April 23, 1993.

5. From Carolyn Staley interview with the author, April 26, 1993.

6. From Tom Campbell interview with the author, April 23, 1993.

Notes for Chapter 3

1. Levin, Robert E., *Bill Clinton: the Inside Story,* S.P.I. Books, New York, NY, 1992, page 116.

2. Quoted in *People Weekly,* February 17, 1992, page 43.

3. Quoted in *Current Biography Yearbook,* H. W. Wilson Co., New York, 1988, page 20.

4. Quoted in Allen and Portis, page 59.

5. See comments regarding this by Hillary Rodham Clinton in *Newsweek,* February 3, 1992.

6. Quoted in Allen and Portis, *Bill Clinton: The Comeback Kid,* Birch Lane Press, New York, 1992, page 36.

Notes for Chapter 4

1. Story as told in *U.S. News and World Report,* July 20, 1992, page 31.

2. Both quotes are from a transcript of Governor Bill Clinton's speech of October 3, 1991 that was provided by President Clinton's Arkansas office.

3. From *Facts on File,* vol. 52, No. 2695, page 519.

4. Quoted in *Clinton: Portrait of Victory,* Warner Books, Inc. 1993, page 119.

Index

Inauguration Day 59, 61
Irons, Edith 13
Kelley, Virginia *see Blythe, Virginia*
Kennedy, John F. 17-19
Kiwanis Key Club 17
Leopoulos, David 8-11, 16, 65, 68
Leverett Elementary School 34, 37
Lincoln, Abraham 23, 56
Little Rock, Arkansas 35, 41, 51
National Governor's Association 47
New Hampshire primary 51
New Orleans, Louisiana 3
Newsweek 11, 65, 68, 69
Nixon, Richard M. 27
Oxford University 23, 51
Perot, H. Ross 54
Perpich, Rudy 47
Purvis, Joe 5
Ramble Elementary School 10
Smith, Caleb 32
Smith, Steve 32
Socks 63, 64
Staley, Carolyn 13, 17, 22, 65, 68, 69
United States Army 51
University of Arkansas 4, 25, 27
Vietnam 27, 51
Washington, D.C. 17-19, 23, 63, 64
Watergate 27
Yale University 24, 27

About the Author

Leslie Kitchen is a historian and journalist who lives in southern California with his nine-year-old daughter, Michelle.

Author photograph.